04916

This book is

KU-160-591

WITHDRAWN FROM
BRENT LIBRARIES

TELEPEN
03146831

THINKABOUT

Big and Little

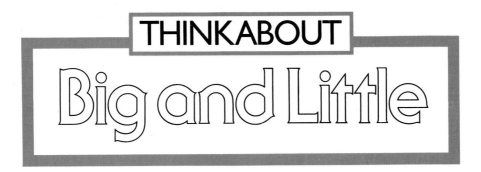

THINKABOUT
Big and Little

Text: Henry Pluckrose
Photography: Chris Fairclough

Franklin Watts
London/New York/Sydney/Toronto

© 1986 Franklin Watts
12A Golden Square
London W1

ISBN: 0 86313 395 9

Editor: Ruth Thomson
Design: Edward Kinsey

Additional Photographs: Zefa

Typesetting: Keyspools

Printed in Italy

LONDON BOROUGH OF BRENT
SCHOOL LIBRARY SERVICE

About this book

This book is designed for use in the home, playgroup, kindergarten and infant school.

Parents can share the book with young children. Its aim is to bring into focus some of the elements of life and living which are all too often taken for granted. To develop fully, all young children need to have their understanding of the world deepened and the language they use to express their ideas extended. This book takes the everyday things of the child's world and explores them, harnessing curiosity and wonder in a purposeful way.

For those working with young children each book is designed to be used both as a picture book, which explores ideas and concepts, and as a starting point to talk and exploration. The pictures have been selected because they are of interest in themselves and also because they include elements which will promote enquiry. Talk can lead to displays of items and pictures collected by children and teacher. Pictures and collages can be made by the children themselves.

Everything in our environment is of interest to the growing child. The purpose of this book is to extend and develop that interest.

Henry Pluckrose.

Do you ever wonder
what words mean?
This is a toy elephant.
It is so big,
that it's difficult to carry.

This baby elephant is bigger than the toy elephant.

These fully-grown elephants
are the biggest of them all.

This is a toy car.

How do you know
that it is too small
to carry people?

This car looks similar
to the toy car.

How can you tell
that it is bigger?

Look at this van.

Is it bigger or smaller
than the car?

This coach carries
lots of people.
It is the biggest of all.

To judge the size of things
we need to see them
close together.

These fruits are different sizes.

Which is the biggest?
Which is the smallest?

These koalas are different sizes too.
Which is the biggest?
Which is the smallest?

These jars are different sizes.

They can be put
in order of size.

The biggest is on the left.
The smallest is on the right.

Do you ever wonder
what words mean?

A rabbit is
bigger than·

a gerbil,

but smaller than a pony.

A pony is smaller than a camel.

What is big?
What is small?

This is a small chair.

But it is bigger
than this doll's house chair.

This chair is bigger.

This chair
is the biggest
of all.

Which chair is
the right size
for teddy?

This child needs
some shoes.
Which ones are too big?
Which ones are
    too small?

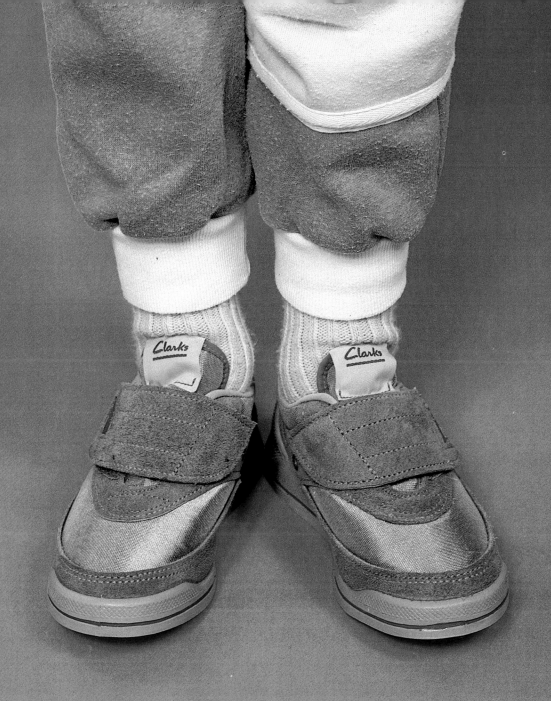

This pair is just the right size!

Find some things
of your own.

Which is the biggest?
Which is the smallest?

Sort them by size.

Perhaps you'll end up
with a pattern like this.

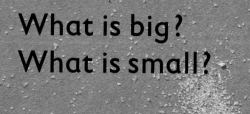

What is big?
What is small?

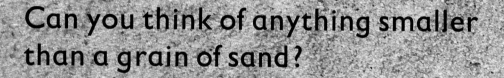

Can you think of anything smaller
than a grain of sand?